LIBERTY STREET HILL

LIBERTY STREET HILL

Poems by

Paul Scollan

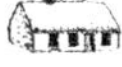

Antrim House

Simsbury, Connecticut

Library of Congress Control Number: 2010922408

ISBN: 978-0-9823970-8-4

Printed & bound by United Graphics, Inc.

First Edition, 2010

Artwork (from oil on canvas paintings) by Neil J. Scollan

Author photograph by Philip Scollan

Book design by Rennie McQuilkin

Antrim House
860.217.0023
AntrimHouse@comcast.net
www.AntrimHouseBooks.com
21 Goodrich Road, Simsbury, CT 06070

Acknowledgments

Grateful acknowledgment to the following publications where poems in this volume first appeared, sometimes in earlier versions:

The Litchfield Review: "Farewell Walk" (as "Widow's Walk"), "Hell and Mrs. Spader"
Oasis Journal: "Bridie," "Liberty Street Hill," "Neighbor Helene's Visit," "Pigeons," "Snapple Bottle"
Sow's Ear Review: "Haircut"
The William and Mary Review: "A Pair of Old Nuns in a Super-Discount Store"

My thanks to Rennie McQuilkin for his support, guidance and, most of all, encouragement.

TABLE OF CONTENTS

THE COURSE OF THINGS

TRIP WIRES

ABOUT THE AUTHOR / 85

*"And so I took the forty-thousand and bought
wood for the woodpeckers."*

- Elizabeth Geelan Scollan

Kicking In

Slaying the Dragon

It wasn't really a dragon:
it was a steep craggy hillock, truth be told,
though to me it could have breathed
fire for the sheer might of it.

It wasn't really the hill, either,
but the quaking dread of dizzying places,
and yet the scaredy-cat in me wasn't enough
to block the want to plant a flag on top.

Pure chicken at first, I went partway up,
went back again, bore down on my tremors
with heart thudding, heart misfiring,
and did it!

Oh, the jubilation that shook the sky that morning,
the ripples that eddied right down to the toes,
in spite of, and so damn much louder than,
the howls of laughter from the climber jocks.

Mr. Engels

Mr. Engels, my high school English teacher,
must have sensed that this waffling wiseacre
kid was turning a corner toward something
besides girls, clowning, loafing and girls
when he didn't make a martyred face on hearing
the class assignment to read everything we could
read by an American author, and mine, he decided,
would be William Faulkner, said, as I recall,
without a smidgen of mischief on his kindly face,
and so in the weeks to follow I fell quiet and unglued,
caught in the pull of the swamps and the blood-run clay
of Mississippi, and come time for the oral presentation,
I was surprised at how I threw myself into it –
all ass, arms and elbows – taking the plunge, gasping for air
through the Yazoo River's sucking mud and undercurrents,
doing my damnedest to make sense of the run-on
lines, the liberties with time, the knotted kinship
of sharecroppers, slave offspring, deluded gentry, misfits,
swimming for all I was worth, near drowning – but at last
making it to the bank on the other side, collapsing
at Mr. Engels' feet, looking up to him beaming a teacher's beam,
grinning the *gotcha* grin of knowing that the potion took hold
but would take its sweet time, delivering the punch someday,
like early one morning over coffee when bone-tired, I am staring
out the kitchen window at the broom-straw maple tapping against
the unopened sky and the last patches of snow sliding downstream,
yesterday closing down so much it's hiding from itself...
when *whoomp!* it kicks in in a way that coffee can't, not even close.

Hell and Mrs. Spader

Our neighbor Mrs. Spader never gave much thought to hell,
as her progressive Methodism gave it only a tiny footnote
and her liberal arts education looked on it as medieval myth
    and metaphor.
In this 1950's blue-collar neighborhood of truck drivers,
    machinists and plumbers,
she and her engineer husband didn't quite fit in,
and wouldn't you know, in a few years they moved to a big
    house on the hill.
My mother, conversely, was as sure there was a hell as there was
    an Akron, Ohio,
or else explain why would it leap from the pages of the Bible
or leap so freely from Father O'Rourke's tongue
as he stoked the furnace fires from the pulpit;
and, besides, out of fairness to the righteous must there be
the dankest den for the heathens and the shameless sinners,
not to forget the English who watched as the Irish starved.
And so, across the rusted wire fence dividing us,
holding armloads of hung wash or fistfuls of plucked weeds,
they held their backyard forum, stiffly cordial,
my mother holding forth as one who had truth
firmly by the throat, not about to let it go;
Mrs. Spader gently chiming the word *mercy* in a litany,
wincing at mention of the fiery Hades, along with the notion
of a wizened old man at the switch of a trap-door to damnation.
I, the acolyte boy, took it all in once
from behind the hemlock, cheering my mother on;
but the scene coming back again and again has

the patch of lawn swept in a carpet of flame,
the two of them throwing down their wet bed sheets,
stomping through the ash and smoke like primitive rain-
    dancers,
and, with the fire finally out, collapsing in utter exhaustion,
embracing each other for all they were worth,
intertwined for always in the risen curls of smoke.

Love Note in a Plastic Ring

Early that morning, putting on my shoe
in the usual harried late-for-work way,
I slipped into one and then the other,
and in the other, the right shoe,
I felt a hard lump under the arch,
reached and found a clear plastic ring,
the kind they use to secure and seal
plastic bottle caps, and I wondered
how could it have gotten there,
and it hit me, the only thing I could –
no, would – come up with:
my wife was twisting off a cap
from a medicine bottle on her dresser;
the ring flew off and landed in the shoe rack
and into my shoe, right next to hers,
and I could see her on hands and knees
looking around for it for some time,
and finally giving up because she was
in the usual harried late-for-work way.
Some accidents lean toward intent – my belief,
and so what came to mind was the rolled love note,
clumsily worded, taped under the desk in geometry class,
or, better yet, a slip of paper written in code
by secret lover spies of the French Resistance,
a postscript of *mon cheri's* added, before being slipped
into book pages in the dusty stacks of a Paris library –
so dearly needing to be read, like this piece of plastic,
which begs to be out – in a harried, late-for-work way.
For me, just as good, for what it was.

Snapple Bottle

No, it wasn't just wet leaves and dewy grass
blinking back the grazing, Indian-summer sun
but a cracked and shattered Snapple bottle, too,
leaning on a tuft of curbstone scruff,
the paper label parted from the barrel,
clear-glass pebbles scattered all around,
winking shimmery along with the sodden grass.

And, as the mind works, a time-reverse took
the bottle swinging backward to the passing car,
to the hand that threw it, the store that stocked it,
the metal hand that made it from a mold;
and, as the mind shirks, the rebound threw it all back,
exact, through the quirky swerves again,
this time to an altered ending
of a kicked-off, glassy slipper from a fleeing lover
and a string of diamonds flung, just touching.

I picked up the daily paper
after clearing up the litter.

Haircut

It was one of those family discount haircut stores
where you get the next of four or five hairdressers.
She was petite, in her early 20's likely,
tattoos of something on her upper right arm,
short-cropped hair dyed orange,
a small ring in her left nostril,
and introduced as Megan,
and I wondered what I had gotten into;
then, without my saying, she told me what I wanted,
correctly, and commenced to move deftly
through my shock of wild Einstein hair,
snipping in neat layers with scissors and comb
as snowy tumbleweed rolled down the dark-blue cape;
and my remark that she seemed a pro
set loose a flow of self-revelation
of wanting to get into graphic arts like her dad
but ending up a hairdresser instead,
practicing on her dad till she got it right,
and how this was art too, wasn't it?
And in no time she was done.
Dropping scissors and comb she picked up her hand-mirror
and flashed back a perfectly-sculpted cut,
saying this was part of her,
and I'd be taking part of her with me.
As I unhooked my jacket and reached for the sleeve,
I looked back to see her sweeping
my hair-clippings into a delicate standing pile
and ever so gingerly picking it up with her fingers
and placing it down under her big-mirror work station,
as if it were a cast-off secondary creation,
just as perfect, from me to her.

Ear Lobes

They're seashells grooved to stream her voice;
they're leathery flaps designed for grip.
We who shrink know oh so well how
mothers from the grave still wag the digit
disapprovingly, and even when we're sure
we squeezed unnoticed through the crack
or missed the bruising pinches on the arm
with air-tight case to sweep us clean,
an unseen hand swoops down to clip the ear
and drag us to the scene of our misdoing,
leaving only one last judgment, hers.
When other times we don our professorial tweeds
and lay excuses out in rows of chalkboard logic,
a chalky figure made of sticks steps out
from jostling crowds of words, erasing the malarkey,
and then, erasers firmly held in both her hands,
administers a clapping to our ears.

Rock-Paper-Scissors

Every kid knows it:
a way to choose up and a game in itself,
a 50-50 split, be it the fist, the two fingers or open hand.
Now, seeing from afar, I'll throw paper:
the rock is too blunt and obtuse,
scissors too single-minded on slashing.
But paper is another matter entirely:
it tears and crumbles under assault,
giving way to the mightier forces,
yet does the trick better than the others;
it prevails by covering the rock's brutal blow,
and gives in to scissors as a gift to geometric design.
As we age we hew to the idea of muffling
all sharpness and anguished commotion;
the paper surrounds with comfort and calm,
and the rare nipping paper-cut is only a gentle reminder
of the greater hurt of forgetting to give, softly.

2546 AD

The cranium was enlarged and elongated,
the torso grown to a plumpish summer squash,
appendages all shriveled, arms and legs dangling
as useless vestiges kept for nostalgia only;
robotic assemblages made no work of locomotion,
no toil for all things graspable needing manipulation.
Such was this world of no sweat, no travail,
no more grinding gears of deliberation and decision,
no untoward feelings, no pain, discomfort or distress,
feelings bothersome or disagreeable caught in the filter,
the spheres of pleasure enhanced to rapture
by pleasure-dome engineers of virtual alternative.

They delivered me, returned me to this world again,
five centuries earlier, to get more practice on the lower rungs,
they said, when instead of being grateful that I'd been tapped
from millions of others for this near-utopia,
I raised my thoughtwaves about the sweet ache of effort –
the strife of striving, the purging sweat of the steep climb,
the bumps and jolts of self-doubt, the weariness of a long walk;
groused about missing the pits in the peaches, the briars in the path,
the fly on my hot dog, the winter cracks bleeding my hands,
working out kinks in my shoulder, shedding tears for tears' sake.
So back I went to the penalty box, the place and time of my origin,
humming a song about being happy, happy with unhappiness.

Paths Crossed

Abandon

Guinness Fleadh, NYC, June 14, 1997

They swept through the gates like channeled water,
pooled in places along the tented grounds;
tomato-slice faces rested on plastic cups,
teased foam from the drying Guinness taps.

The boy from Cape Breton, the boy with the bow,
gave long and hot chase to his fiddle,
caught the spark that torched the tent
from Manhattan's stand of distant lights.

The reels flew faster, wheeled on a swivel;
the loaded bursts popped out of their joints;
they danced alone, they danced in circles,
long after the fiddler split hairs on his bow.

Grim-faced, intent, deaf to the fest,
the trashman poked his stick at the papers,
wove through the crowd gone mad with dance,
his gaze to the litter by the kicking feet.

Four high-stepping girls ringed him round,
never saw the pique that died in his eyes,
just the smile and the graceful unbending,
the wistful salute to abandon.

Wedge of Blacktop

All they could wish was this wedge of blacktop
by the back-porch stoop of this matchbox cape
in this shirt-cling evening of a dog-day swoon,
the breadloaf radio set out on the rail,
the longneck beers, dead soldiers on the stairs,
Blanche kicking high in her grease-stained housedress,
her great girth tweaking like she's traveling light,
Chaz winging free right into tomorrow
in his busman's pants and his spit-shined shoes,
a sleeveless top – and sweet jazz in his moves
to the toot of Duke in "It don't mean a thing,"
and a switch of the dial to slow it all down,
to home them into arms ringing round
to a doo-wop tune could melt chrome
from the Chevy.

Penguins

All colors, sizes, body builds,
these penguins, and there goes
one now, waddling into Walmart
in low-slung pants with way-low crotch
that crimps his stride to mini-steps;
to add to that, the cap, it goes a sideway slant
that could be jaunty if not a bit cartoon-like,
and the shirt so loose and baggy, looking like
a wrestler's cape on a toddler's coat hanger,
arms and neck mapped in squiggly ink,
speaking in code, a sacred creed.

There he is again, milling about in the parking lot
with three others who look just like him;
they roll their shoulders, hit hands, hug fiercely,
laugh softly with smooth grace, their sneakers
gliding in a jive on the patch of ice around them
and past the orderly crowd of parked cars;
they edge toward the curb and beyond to a retaining wall
that drops ten feet down to a shelf of traprock;
they perch, look below from their ledge,
sneer at gravity, the ice, or any regard of ours.

A Pair of Old Nuns in a Super-Discount Store

Side by side the ancients padded,
pushing plastic shopping carts,
both crowned in white starched wimple
flowing black from veil to skirt
to sneakers velcro-strapped, just like
the ones top-shelf in Aisle Two.
No look of passing tourists holding noses
on their descent to the valley of Gomorrah;
instead, of breakaway schoolgirls on a lark,
twinkle-eyed through waxy, vein-webbed faces
that, eyes excepted, were put to rest years ago.
One, and then the other, reached palms-up
as if to catch a snowflake falling, then their hands
turned to form bird beaks so to snatch the prizes
hung on metal prongs. Glazed-over, they peered
into clear plastic domes that enshrined red ribbons,
can openers, silver coasters, manicure kits,
and glided fingertips across the smooth contours
and ridges glinting in the overhead fluorescence.
They sighed in unison as if rehearsed,
and it carried the lilt of a wishful prayer:
Forgive us, Lord,
for asking that the Great Reward also
have a back-lot store in a low-rent block
where shelves stay full
of trifles and sundries everywhere –
such glorious Miscellaneous, just like this.

Pipes Calling

Too young at thirty-one, this stumbling drunk,
but father was, mother was, and more's the pity,
for he'd be long on virtue but for this vice,
with a smile could crack light through the vaulted darkness
and charm the devil himself to acts of kindness,
and, oh my, did that boy love to ride the shiny painted pinto,
to hear the up-and-down glide of the calliope,
lean to one side and then the other,
hang low and lower without slipping his grip
and go limp from the lift of weightlessness
as the sun blurred green in the running trees
and the tune piped fast from the panting crowd,
till, with years and too many, he'd lose his touch,
fall fast and hard to the unmoving ground,
to be tossed to the tank, the dry-out tank,
and let go for another go-round.
But soon, one day, he'd find the off-switch
at three or four or maybe one more,
ride the beast like a Sioux warrior –
and softly dismount. One day.

Doomed from the Womb

Doomed from the womb,
say shrink and worker,
came down both sides of the color line,
and that not enough,
had a mama babbling to voices inside,
papa so drunk he'd answer her babble,
and this boy weaving between them
in quick step from sense to nonsense,
in unwitting mourning with every hairpin turn,
fell down for good in the night-train groove
that shunned every squint of needling sun,
dove down as a mole-like soul shrinking
from the cries of the schoolyard taunts,
and they tugged his tether in the homes and the schools,
sprawled him out on the –ologist's slab,
pumped him with serums, coaxed down the pills
to clear his head of mama's head-patter,
though the patter was all ever greeted him,
ever promised him the grail of sense-bearing life,
this sticky-eyed scamp still licking at the light,
still heaping his helping of crack and booze.
Doomed from the womb.

Five-by-Nine-Foot Cell

Was cold, damp and windowless,
this five-by-nine-foot cell,
with a dirt floor he laid in flagstone
and concrete steps going up to the shrubs
outside his new kitchen addition –
which was the best he could do
with a house never big enough,
now straining at the joists and risers
as his seven ran the span of teen years.

In what could have been a root cellar,
he placed a small stool and a table
with a homemade chessboard on it,
a work light that dangled from a nail overhead,
and steel-frame shelving along the side and back walls,
lined with National Geographics and a set of Collier's,
and shelf-space set aside for a few jars of peanuts
and a tall bottle of Tullamore Dew.

On those days when the din rose to a high,
he would retire to his hole in the ground,
map the moves of Fischer and Spasski,
visit China's emperor buried with his terra-cotta army
and nod to the gods on a sip of their dew.
The day very rarely came,
what with the drag and pull of his life;
that it was there
was all that mattered,
waiting beneath the floorboards,
his five-by-nine-foot cell.

Sincerity

Greta's in to see the shrink, her first,
this willowy Nordic blonde of thirty-five,
a stunning beauty, nature unassisted:
her mouth plump-red and dark,
her blues chipped out of ice from glacier walls,
a smooth-glow skin above the shadow falling,
a grace that lunched a thousand lips
yet stranger to love's lasting aftertaste.
From wealthy gentlemen to sexy, many,
she never let the hurting turn on her,
right through the cutting blades without a scratch.

Asked about ever having a true friend,
she says yes, a *gal-pal* once, two kindred spirits,
so she thought, only to find that she was being played
as shill to draw them in at singles bars.

Calico Cat

I.

As with so many others stuck in the broom closet,
this one, too, started out befriended, all eyes and ears
tuned to a creature stuffed.
Hers was Cal the calico cat, popped-out button eyes,
a burst seam-hole with innards coming out, the nap
worn smooth as a baby's rump bathed and powdered.
But when the thunder rolled across the kitchen floor,
Cal fell into the arm's wrap, soothing-strong
in comfort, in making the thumping go soft
and the crashing noises fade to a trickle. Then –
the change, exactly when, she didn't know:
first, no more smell of fresh laundry soap
but the dank odor of driveway oil rag instead;
next, not always being there at hand's reach, and over time
getting lost many times and recovered, then lost forever,
this constant companion. To do this, to leave her flat,
she thought, Cal must have been held captive,
or fitted with devilish horns, sharp hidden teeth
and a tough leather hide, just like grownups.

II.

Dad went wherever, so no more yelling and hitting,
no burning breath, no sweat, no stubbly chin, holey tee shirts;
Mom went back to the sick-smelling gin, swigging it dry, till
her tongue went thick, her face red, and flames licked her open lips.
But before long came other men with bristly beards, dirty tee shirts,

again the screaming, yelling, we kids trying to hide but no places;
one bed for sleep, a mattress on the floor – brother, sister, me –
Mom spinning around, tilting fast, on a slow totter before
going down with the bottle breaking, silence breaking even louder.
And all we had to hold was each other, reaching over, hanging on
till the skirt-lady broke us up and put us in stranger-homes for a while,
and back again with Mom, and it wasn't long before
I had a growing itch to run at 13, wishing it so hard
it sprouted wings and swept me up like my gin-spinning Mom.
So off I flew from this northern mill town to the Texas panhandle,
and life was good – for a good while, till the next need to escape.

Aggie's Office Visit

Aggie guided her shoulder along the office wall
and never really came to rest on the office chair,
her fingers threading a needle never there,
and, try as she would,
couldn't begin to shake her wrists
free of the razor-thin scars
fastened like old stripped feathers
well past shedding,
nor could she squeeze a tear
from the well deep within,
for each one dried up
before the fresh droplet formed,
and her mouth overworked with pleading
below the lowly brood of her eyes.
There was no such food yet, I knew,
to nourish, savor, or fill.
Her skin held the stamp of the crow's feet,
pulled tightly in a dim seal –
a fading parchment about to tear.
In one rare moment she flushed with warmth
when a quaint irony amused her,
then stopped dead in her smile,
embarrassed, reaching for composure.

The record on her read that
age fifteen she hurtled her body five stories
from a tenement roof in St. Louis
as Mom looked on through the sooty window
and Mom's stranger lover woke up startled.

The doctors did wonders,
for she was up and walking in no time.
She must have dreamed herself a pinwheel
beating the air, whirling ahead to this peculiar *now*,
the dream and the dreamer folded over to one.
She never stopped falling and hitting hard surfaces,
but one day she'd master amazing stunts:
dive with flawless precision,
break and cushion falls with ease,
spring to her feet, walk away,
and shake it all off.

Bridie

The phone rang.
My mother answered.
It was Bridie calling to chat,
the third time this week,
so unlike quiet, shy Bridie,
who one day was drying peat near the River Shannon,
the next scrubbing floors in this New England factory town,
married a French-Canadian lumberjack-turned-butcher,
gave light to a brood of nine in about as many years,
all scampering over one another in that matchbox house,
stacked up like cordwood at bedtime,
and the old man suddenly dying before they were grown,
Bridie still stirring the big pot,
looking after each with those strong, cracked-dry hands,
and, as life would have it, in no time they were gone
to wedding and religious vows, sworn oaths to Uncle Sam,
fine sons and daughters all –
and Bridie alone in the matchbox house.

She kept talking on the phone,
reminiscing about the kids' childhood shenanigans
and our Friday-night gatherings after food shopping,
her lilting brogue quickening, rising to exuberance
as my mother's pot boiled over
and the potatoes burned in the oven,
and, finally, Bridie took the cue, hanging up.

And little did we know then
that she resumed her chatter,

not a beat missed,
with a guest, a regular, at the kitchen table,
a barrel-chested man with a calming hand,
a bellhop's fez cap, a bobbing bow tie
above a black vest with shiny brass buttons
that shimmered and spun in the light through the curtains.

First on the Scene

They raced each other home from the fourth grade,
Brendan and his twin brother Nathan,
crashed through the back door,
their feet barely touching the floor,
plopped their sheaves of schoolwork on the kitchen table,
turned on their heels and hydroplaned out the door,
with Brendan first on the scene
at Reuben's house three houses down,
Reuben the sheepdog, tied to a dog-run a backyard long.
The giant pup leaped and yipped joyfully on seeing them;
they played and chattered for the longest time,
Reuben snapping up each word and gesture as if a biscuit.

Twenty more years of wear on the kitchen table,
and Brendan's NYPD gym bag on it,
lightly packed for a weekend visit home
after two weeks of extra double shifts
with the 23rd Precinct, Spanish Harlem.
A smile and quick greeting under heavy lids,
he excused himself as he slowly trudged up the stairs
to take a nap in his old bedroom;
came down three hours later, refreshed,
and made himself a sandwich.
Work was going okay, he offered between bites,
and went quiet for a while
before adding that it got busy a few nights ago:
a call to a fourth-floor apartment in the projects –
man shot dead through the head, drug-gang style,
and the gunpowder still in the air on arrival,
and it seeped, then and there, into our kitchen.
First on the scene.

Little Jimmy Grayson

In the back of his head,
over and over,
goes the wind-up, the pitch,
the sound of bad wood.

From the boardroom's oak walls
he hears the same thing,
no crisp crack of the bat,
just the cough of bad wood.

Was Little Jimmy Grayson once,
cut from the peewee team
for all the swung misses,
the dribbles in the dirt.

Now he's sixty and mighty,
owns a Major League team
which fills up the ballpark,
wins him game after game –

all the more to confound him,
this little conundrum,
that in his head he still hears
the sour note of bad wood.

Bigot

This time it was the Mexicans
as target for the target shoot.
Standing another beer can on the fence post,
he stepped back ten paces
and commenced to fire away
about his two years in Corpus Christi
running a hotel laundry sweatshop
with all those people, "those wetbacks,"
who'd screw in their cars on lunch break,
smoke pot in the john, carry knives in their sock,
pick your pocket if you didn't watch it,
get soused after work and beat their wives silly.
No one had a name. No Rafael, Carmen or Joaquin.
Nothing about the ancestral empire built on a lake.
No mention of passion-songs about *palomas*
that ache and yearn with the rapture of beating wings.

Back from the men's room, his gun still smoking,
the shooter looked around for his buddies
as he ordered another beer,
but his audience was gone and the beer was flat.
He looked into the vast mirror behind the bar
and had to tilt his head to free his face
from the space between two whiskey bottles.

Sitz Baths

The tour guide took us through the bathroom
of the Vanderbilt summer mansion on the cliffs,
marble all around us, the bathtub sculpted
from a two-ton block, two sitz baths on the opposite wall,
anatomically scooped to accommodate the derriere,
there for their comfort, we were told, after a long day
of posterior punishment from horseback riding or polo.
Sometimes they would get stuck
and one of their forty servants would help them out.
My grandmother Brigid, an Irish housemaid for a Yankee family
during this era, wouldn't have curbed her tongue,
and at risk of dismissal would have muttered something the likes of,
"A fat arse is a fat arse no matter,
and sooch an insult to sooch a fine stone."

Servants' Quarters

We had to see The Breakers while there,
friends said, and so we took the tour
of the Vanderbilt Palazzo on the cliffs,
shepherded through stands of alabaster
and marble columns, mosaics, gold brocade,
tapestries, drapes of silk and velvet,
carved woods from Africa and distant continents,
under chandeliers and stained-glass skylight,
all the finest artistry imaginable,
the cavernous Great Hall to rival the Taj Mahal,
an upper loggia with a view that owned the sea,
in its heyday forty servants moving about unheard,
inconspicuous as chameleons, in this castle by the sea –
the grandeur of it all taking my breath away.

The upper-floor stairway was cordoned off.
Were the servants' quarters up there,
I wondered, and found a docent in the corner
and she said, yes, they were in the attic, in cubbies
just wide enough for bed and chamber pot,
just enough room to squeeze between bed and wall.

And the breath that was taken away was taken back
all at once, and it pressed very hard against my lips.

Tough to Tender

The first time Dee lost her counselor's cool,
she crossed paths with the prowling wolf
who fed on her lost lamb Tara,
the one she pulled from the brambles,
just like the Good Shepherd in the church hymnal picture,
only these brambles were the tight wrapping fingers
of the drug-baited traps and their guardians,
and so, unthinking, Dee bowed her head as if in prayer
but raised curving, pointed horns instead,
ripped into the wolfman by the door,
poured her scorn, laid him bare as Tara never could,
and at that moment Dee was her dad,
the gritty, leathery Montana rancher
who gave her her heart and her righteous ire,
as when Billy Red Sky bad-touched her sister
and saw the look he knew to fear,
the lowered crown of the rageful bison,
and in this manner father stood, shotgun cradled,
sent him scampering, never to cross that line again,
this Crow brother from the Crow *rez*,
from brothers he shared land with, gave banned whiskey to,
went hunting with, to thin out the herd,
whose wind-mapped skin and noble high cheekbones
were in his face, and Dee's, too.

The second time she lost it
they rolled her Tara out on a gurney
after her OD on crack and booze
sent her into howls of contempt,
My addiction! My addiction!

ringing down the long hallway,
and in the unsettling calm that followed,
Dee came sobbing from behind the office door,
took a breath for breathing air,
smoothed and straightened herself,
and carried on with business.

Liberty Street Hill

I.

Starting mid-October the early-morning sun
rolls to a stop at the crest of Liberty Street hill
and levels a dagger-point glare
into the eyes of the climbing driver,
blinding him for at least three or four seconds,
and even those prepared with shades and windshield visor
are struck nearly helpless for all their effort,
as with our neighbor, Old Man Hannigan,
never one to blink at anything never mind the sun,
having to pull off the road one day,
and wouldn't you know he jumped with a start
from his recliner later that night
after nodding off with the TV on,
and swore he felt the screen's flash slice his chest
like the hooded reaper himself with the swinging scythe.

II.

Nogales, Chicago's south side, now this Connecticut factory town.
Marisol feels the sun's warmth on the back of her sweatshirt
as she walks down Liberty on her way to school,
one hand clutching the strap of her backpack,
the other snatching a falling red maple leaf,
and she stops to feel the waxy skin and the fragile rib cage,
and sees its skeleton as she holds it up to the light,
all the while wincing inside with last night's image
of the crimson trickle down her thigh,

Aunt Carmen's brown starfish hands talking
of womanhood, the gift of life-giving, eggs waiting
for the man's mount and the shooting seeds.
She sees herself pushing away Aunt Carmen and the panting man
for her moon landing sideways through her bedroom curtain,
brightly onto the rumpled bed sheets and the dark valleys in the folds
where she sits alone, waiting for it to curl up into her lap.

Farewell Walk

I. Spring

At twenty-nine he's got a wife, two kids,
a life to live, a tumor sitting in his brain
(what's left of what the doctors couldn't get),
here before me to be counseled
how to talk to It the next two years or four or six
by this old man with sixty-one,
who shook his hand, did proper introductions,
bit down hard inside to hold back platitudes
and soothing words that carry comfort sickly.
Sensing this he grinned, leaned forward in the sofa,
doffed his Red Sox cap and cursed his losing team,
mocked a smile while pointing to the train-track scars
that crossed his short-cropped skull – and just as fast
he put It back beneath the bright-red lid
so not to tumble down and rattle round the room,
and take me with It, murderous jokester that It was.

II. Summer

With six months passing to August
came three easy, thumbs-up rounds of chemo
that squeezed the ball of rogue cells
to pea-size, to mind their own business – for now;
and with another six months passing
came a new Mickey,
the comeback kid with the *now* look
of designer tee shirt and pierced ear,
gel-spiked hair that hid the worm drawn by the knife.

And when no one was looking, it happened:
he leapfrogged back in time to the stops missed,
reached through the threadbare shroud beside him
and pulled up a circus tent with yellow banners waving
on a summer day that wouldn't stop unfolding
clover fields into honeysuckle climbing a roadside fence,
hair flying in tangles of laughter from the open Ford convertible,
moonlight grazing the pressed-flower skin in the back seat,
the slap of the catcher's mitt from the dust storm at home plate,
watermelon sliced dripping-red on the shaded picnic table,
the pond splash under the rope swing still swinging,
the blooming handful of cotton candy on the walk down the midway,
and back to the Barnum and Bailey tent, roaring, elephants trunk-to-tail.
Sitting across from me, sinking into the sofa,
he said his head didn't hurt anymore
and the fog was clearing,
but strange that his mind was so crowded with things *summer* –
bird's-eye scenes, scraps of memory, déjà vu's –
and having described them said he wanted to go back
again and again, to have each generate a new one
inside the old one that just flashed.
With that he paused a long pause before saying
he didn't care where it came from,
this summer obsession, whether poisoned brain cells,
a trick of the mind, or death-defying denial –
he wasn't going to let it go.
Session ended, I walked him outside to a light snowfall;
the snowflakes fell all around him but not on him.

III. Winter

Another six months brought another round of chemo,
much more potent stuff this time, a cocktail of trial drugs
to block the advance of the rogue cells
that by now had set up shop in the memory center.
Six more ushered in another Mickey,
absent two months for memory rehab
and carrying thirty extra pounds thanks to steroids,
his hair uncombed and matted, no more earring,
no Red Sox emblems or team colors,
no lit-up look on meeting me (my name still on his lips, thankfully).
He smiled with assurances he was handling things okay,
though the forgetting thing sure was a bitch,
and he handed me the reminder pad with a message from family
about mood, weight, interactions with family, memory –
and, below that, reminders to him to dress, brush teeth, shower, etc.
He talked about the chemo, wife, kids, daily routine,
and repeated his litany every ten minutes or so;
no hint of summer, not the faintest glimpse,
even with summer in the window as prompter.
Our meeting over, I mumbled ineptly about hanging in there,
shook his hand and walked him outside to the waiting car.

Balance

It wasn't hand, eye, reflex,
bicycle or road below that failed him,
no, none of those, when he fell
to the sidewalk on his way home
from work in the big city.
It was the virus that had wormed
its way into the brain where the nexus
of balance lay, we later learned.
For him the utter bewilderment:
the sudden vertigo, there on the sidewalk,
face-down, the bicycle thrown along the curb,
the wheels still spinning, the great
spheres cockeyed on their axes.

Hanging on to the curbside sapling,
he slowly rose to his feet, shaken
to the depths of him, the self-correcting
gyro gone haywire, no longer assisting
the navigator, bringing an end
to all he knew and the start to a long roll
of hospital wards, visiting nurses,
filled pill boxes, family scrambling and
dumbly standing by, some of them walking
into three rapid-fire punches – gay, AIDS, dying.

He leaned on the cane, suddenly into late-age,
turning from the thoughts that fly to fear:
of judgment, retribution, narrow footpaths
for the righteous, mother's reproach, Sodom,
Sister Maura's starched wimple, deadly sins

coiled like tapeworms, squared certitude,
the catechism's crisp answers – all now afoul
with man and man together, the unutterable,
seraphim turning into gargoyles, all falling down
on the priest-ridden forebears, falling down,
the impact, the hydrant, the no-parking
sign, the crack in the curb shooting
grass, the jagged teeth on beer-bottle
glass, down there where the broom sweeps.

Benny

It was dinner call at the The Meadows.
Slowly they tottered, barely moving in the hall,
propped on canes, walkers, wheeling themselves in chairs,
shepherded with *c'mon dears* by young aides in white.
She didn't know yet that I was there visiting,
that through the door-crack I could see her
sitting there alone in the *rec* room,
deaf to dinner call, all ears to the music
of Benny and his band from the speaker-box behind her,
tootling horn as fleet as a Jesus Lizard on water-feet.
Her smile grew and her body flew to it,
legs bouncing, crimped hands clapping her thighs –
that once plunked piano jigs to her papa's fiddle,
keyed up parties threatening to go dull,
the same that tended rows of diapers, raised a brood,
broke daily bread near the priest's table,
rolled beads to restore her mother's strength.
And so I left her alone with Benny for a while,
and waited in the chapel, her other favored place,
where she'd pray early mornings for another evening
to hear the swing from Benny in the room across the way,
for the reckoning had come, all the earthly work was done,
and now was the time for God's sublime in the room across the way.

Salute to Harry Coons

There he'd be, with that wobbly gait,
rumpled polo shirt tucked into oversized polyester pants,
scuffed walking shoes with laces trailing,
at the crown of his head a thatch of hair
going this way and that to say the hell with ya,
eyebrows bushy as squirrel tails, and through clicking teeth
would greet all strangers, even peers, as *young man, young woman,*
and would tell stories of his younger days
as if they'd happened for the telling alone,
marking the high points with a floor-thump of his cane,
and give a loud cackle for the finishing touch,
no matter how happy or sad the ending.
At parades he was most alive, stood there beaming,
wearing his army piss-cutter cap with medals dangling,
and when it came time for taps at the flagpole,
he'd make a funny grimace meant to hold back tears;
drove a big Olds with long bench seats,
his "Ark de Triumph," which turned in a small lot
like a battleship in a small inlet of kayaks;
would sneak to the tool shed for a nip of sour mash
to spite his bossy daughter and prune-faced Dr. Owens;
would order useless junk through the mail,
drop intimacies at the bathroom mirror,
talk to the dead he'd visit in his head
or in the boneyard where his buddies went;
feed stray cats, pick up hitchhikers,
drop a fin for Charlie who tented in the woods,
pass time with legless Hanna out to air on her porch,
go home to sleep like a stone at the bottom of the sea
and wake to greet the morning star with a wink,
and it'd always wink back, he'd say, always.

Neighbor Helene's Visit

Seeing it now, only months later,
she gasped for air, held herself
steady on the linden out front,
let it wash over her many long seconds,
then, recovering, went back to it,
this house once hers,
before her now a melt of day-lily yellows,
all come together in sash, shutter and clapboard.

Count the years to a half-century
of this house and slice of lawn and garden,
theirs till his passing, then hers alone
all those years till parting with it, and with life at 85.
Near the end, the hearing, vision going,
her Germanic sense of order, too,
the legs locking as she padded along peeling kitchen walls,
the birdfeeder hanging empty from the flowering crab,
the flower beds untended, transom on all that was lovely –
her peeking trillium, her climbing clematis.

Moving round back, she gasped again,
a riptide sluicing through her veins
and rising up to weigh against her chest.
She took it in: the mounds of dirt,
the backhoe, chainsaw, limbs piled high,
the fence torn loose, the shed where once the garden was.
Back those eyes rolled to welcome the night,
but just before the silence wrapped her full,
she trapped a crack of summer lit up in the grass
and in it put a goldfinch threading
arbor vines of morning glory –
to tightly hold it, take it with her for the trip.

Neighbor Dorothea

The way she told the last one
she could have been sitting at the kitchen table,
tapping a Pall Mall to pack it
before lighting a clear path to the story
for my mother stirring the dinner pot for her brood:
the one about the neighbor kid stuck under the fence,
or the squirrel intruder in her bedroom.
But, instead, this was her deathbed,
and she told it as it unfolded,
her eyes half-closed, her listeners all around,
the words still smooth and trim as her packed Pall Mall,
there, standing on the hillside, sleep-talking
of the deepest stone-moss green,
white streamer clouds on a sky burgundy red,
and she was calling the missing,
opening her arms to her crib-dead son,
her long-gone husband, her mother, father, brother,
sitting them down in the cool evening grass
to tell her story of days without them.

Cradle Grave

Didn't know him at all,
though he lived only a few houses down.
Word has it he was born and raised
in that same house, saw his parents
to their end, never married,
remained there all his working years
to retirement and to his own death
in that same modest house,
and avoided eye contact
in passing me on the walk.
That's all I know, except –
two weeks before he died
he was outside every evening,
leaning on the porch rail,
very pensive, eyes glazed,
even waved hello once,
and kept looking out to the rooftops
as if, before going, he wanted to break
through the hard, layered walls of his heart,
to throw himself into the dreaded riptide
and let it sweep him out to the Great Whatever
he hid from, to be washed away to the hope
of arms waiting, outstretched, the menace relaxed.

The Course of Things

Poetry

The knotted string of snow geese sweeping the icy ridge-spine,
the soft-sloped hummock of a sleeping cat's back,
a bride bending down to gather up her gown,
a teacher's chalky hand looping letters,
the merciful, oblique approach of sea rain
come through the whiteness here in floating cursive.

Pigeons

There must have been twenty or more of them on the wire,
divided evenly on sides of the telephone pole,
adding a crosspiece of their own to the tall upright
risen over the house-rows, a bar and a hair salon;
wing-to-wing and plump as turnips,
they hung there with heads sunk in breasts of feathers,
as if free flight forced a need for introspection.
We wonder why they hug the pole,
and the answer comes back as:
they've learned the closer to the pole
the more stable the wire for sitting,
and the cylindrical transformer hums
a motherly warmth they can't resist.
They know their wings cannot support a sky
that keeps opening on itself,
no chance of rest or roost or place to die,
and so they hunker into the limbless tree
for the long leg driven deep down
into an immense whitening cloud
that never lets go.

Taking a Break

I stopped to watch them overhead,
a flock of pigeons wrapped around
a sharp-shinned hawk, banking
in tight circles, flowing
downward like poured water
around their lone foe,
who'd lost power
by their being in the air,
their high level of alert,
their growing numbers.

Oh, I know nature
must have its way
with offense and defense,
killer and killed,
but something was different about this:
both seemed to be taking a break,
not trying very hard, maybe even
taking pleasure, making a game
of chaser and chased –
by the hawk hanging around longer
than necessary, and the pigeons going loose,
going lax in their business of harassing,
and this for some time, maybe minutes,
before the hawk took his leave, slowly.

What Wicked

What wicked, dabbling teaser sun
would practice fire on basking trout,
and in the parting of the leaves,
flash crazily to stands of fern,
so rudely take me from my thoughts?

Copperhead

It was the path I always ran,
beside the lake, between the trees.
I slowed in places to a walk
to take in all around me –
the smell of fern, the rotting bark, the pine needles,
the stitching of finches through the knotted shrubs.
This day on passing from the shade,
I stopped – across the trail a sunning snake,
across its back a running flame,
a copperhead of striking color, poise.
I stood entranced, could not let go.
It moved at last, languorous, through the brush
and dropped beneath the scattered leaves
so deftly brushed aside
by genius waxing softly through.

Fling

From the rusted fence to the chestnut trunk
to the cross-barred window at Bo's Bodega,
yellow crime-scene tape is draped in festive *U's*
from last night's fling.

But it's early next morning
and the catbird perches to clear her throat.

October

Ashes browning, needles bedded,
the breath of old black ale;
winter's thinning summer's blood,
reddish in the sumac's feathers,
dreadful in the lay of mottled mosses,
in the stands of silver maple pluming a demise
on sky too blatant, too untoward for sky.
There's mayhem
in the drowned, bedraggled knapweed
flinging random seeds to feed the air.
The oak leaf teeters on a string,
never touching down.

Anxiety

It rained for nine days straight.
The waters came,
and the river spilled over its banks
and washed over the floodplains.
Day and night we fought back,
sandbagging the levees,
shoring up the dikes with dirt,
always keeping one eye to the sky,
the other to the water level.
It stopped at last,
the water dropped,
and we breathed easier.

The river stayed tame within its banks,
the floodplains remained dry for seasons,
yet I kept pacing the walkway on the bridge
and the path along the levee.
The sandbags were piling up in my sleep;
those are my hands stacking them;
that's the sweat trapped under my poncho;
that's the groaning of the trees as they bend
against the wall of onrushing water.

And so I built me a house on stilts,
high above the sprawling floodplains,
towering legs of steel and concrete.
From my perch I kept watch on the river
bending with each notch on God's crooked finger.
The sight of rain brought a shudder still;

the breaking sunlight brought thin solace.
My prayers went out, straining to take hold
of the Master's jutting hand –
fear's size moving to guide
the course of things to come.

Factory Town

The late-day sun tilts low on the factory walls,
leaves long glowing fuses for telephone lines,
blades running fire for railroad tracks;
red bricks made redder sweat out
the faded names of dead merchants and their sons;
a half-peeled orange sits with its peeled skin
on the green bench of the station platform
as the departing train whistles back;
in the cracked, sun-streamed window
of a long-vacant barber shop next door,
flecks of dust mingle and feud in a whirl
above the tape-repaired barber's chair;
the sunlight shimmers along the sidewalk
and passes over my walking feet
onto small round faces the color of caramel
and to the soccer ball the children are kicking
below the porch steps of the multifamily.
Up the hill stands a grand old lady of a house,
her paint pulling away, the lower windows boarded;
a golden braid of sun comes undone
from the dormer facing west,
dropping below the eaves and soffits,
stealing across the gravel drive,
slipping out of sight.

Birthday Balloon

It was purple, a birthday balloon on a string,
snagged in the brush by the wooded trail,
went a mile from the nearest home,
an aimless journey, likely,
after breaking loose from its moorings,
tied, could be, to a mailbox in front
of the house where the party was held,
a little girl standing over a cake,
seven candles burning brightly,
making her wish with eyes tightly closed,
blowing hard with wistful breath,
and up it flew and flew, and down it went,
to bob between a peeling cedar trunk
and a boulder jutting up from the snowy ground.

Trip-Wires

Gift

On in-country maneuvers outside the base camp,
about twenty of us, all FNG's (Fuckin' New Guys),
moved slowly, skittishly, outside the concertina wire,
our heads crackling with the power of small hidden things
they warned us about, all the *friendly* unexploded ordnance,
trip-wires to booby traps, and the dreaded Bouncing Betty,
a spring-loaded mine that, when tripped, pops up to groin-level,
taking not only the legs but the rest, and your buddies too.
As fresh arrivals to *Nam*, to this division up north,
we were strangers, just a motley team of infantry grunts,
chopper mechanics, desk jockeys, medics – and one cook
I got to know that morning.
Humping for an hour or so, we reached a small hill looking down
into a shallow ravine with a stream bending through it;
we took a rest after forming a perimeter position.
I was the only one not carrying a weapon, just a radio
on my back. We took in the deep rolling green, the sound
of trickling water, the curious taste of irony in the beauty of it.
The cook, a 40-ish lifer from Kentucky with a big beer gut
and a bigger smile, stood by me with his M-16 tightly gripped,
telling a little about himself and the home he found in the Army.
He asked why I had no weapon, and I told him about anti-war
convictions, about hailing from Connecticut, drafted on
    finishing college.
I braced for the lashing to come – a blistering fusillade
about being a yellow Yankee hippy, undeserving of the uniform.
But – it never came. Instead, he said he'd stand by me
with his M-16, just in case something happened.

Cleanup Detail

Was the war that unglued him,
said family and friends,
and the army of shrinks agreed;
it was their drugs that defused him,
gutted the miles of brain circuitry,
dimmed the senses to a flicker,
tamping down the few warm strands left,
and all the aimless strivings,
the volleys misfired into the air,
were no more, were snuffed out
by a pressing weariness come too soon.
They'd silenced the eloquence of falling.

He was living out of his car now,
eating at fast-food joints,
but barely able to hold it down,
or the cheap wine that used to bring sleep.
Was always like this, or so it seemed.
There were jobs once, white-collar jobs,
a condo and a late-model car as well,
but always under the tracking shadow
of a hand waiting to snatch them away,
and the remains, though few, the ex-wives picked over,
looking for something unbroken, untainted.

Was eighteen, only eighteen,
when they dropped him in the mountain clearing;
for a while he was fine, was handling it well,
until, after a night of fire and thunder,
they sent him out on cleanup detail.

Between ragged stalks in the advancing calm,
torn sacks of grain heaved from the ground,
bags of meal that shifted their load
when he shouldered them
like the ones from the barn loft
that summer he worked on the farm.
Some slipped, with sighs gave up their heft,
then rested limply on his arms and neck.

As they told him later,
for he could barely remember,
he kept going back to look for more,
even when it was clear there were no more,
and he wouldn't stop looking
until they ordered him at gunpoint.

R&R, Taipei

Her name Sung Lee, the seer in the dark,
the madam-barkeep of this Taipei bar.
For her the hands told all, and not a hand
got by the grasp of her uncanny eye:
she saw the rank, the work, the manner bred,
their claim to objects, how the fingers spoke,
how fast they burned the wad of riffled bills.

The troops rolled in, two dozen to the bar,
these stumbling boys still new at playing men;
they reared back on their heels with burning stem
as ladies sidled up for evening's catch.
They told their stories, slow as pushing stones:
that night the ambush failed, they ate the dirt
and held his body whole till choppers came,
met Charlie in his maze of spider holes
and counted double for the body count.

Back when, Sung Lee could grasp the GI slang,
could see through the flak vest to a mother's son,
but soon they all left handprints marred the same
across the bartop, tables – all who came.

The Handsome Black Case

In a place where ceremony had no place,
the honor fell on me to confer
this award, this medal for gallantry,
tucked away in a handsome black case in my hand,
to flag him down, this chopper pilot
passing through base camp on his way
to hop a big silver bird back to *The World*,
who flew all those rescue missions
in his unarmed *medevac* chopper machine,
stopped counting holes in his metal skin after the third,
kept nosing it down to the fire-breathing jungle floor,
the rounds snapping around his pedaled feet,
the ribbed hulk seizing and shuddering as it dropped
as his crew chief clambered through curse-flecked prayers,
and the limp, wet parcels waited below
for hands to load them on.

They pointed him out, the one climbing into the jeep,
no toughened, thick-veined warrior before me
but a curly-headed kid with barely a whisker,
and the eyes' awful look of sadness postponed
for an Indiana farmboy-turned-flyboy,
who finished with a thank-you in his smile,
a wave-off of the precious black case
and a turn on the heel.
"Don't need that, man – I'm goin' home,"
was all he said, was all.

There it is, Holmes

There it is, Holmes, was the phrase
that made the *clunking* sound
the cola can makes when it hits
the drop-slot in the vending box –
hip, 'Nam GI talk for payload, pay dirt,
the comeback to put the affirmative
on the dead-on declaration,
no need for explaining.
"Just 27 days 'til I'm back in *The World,*
so gotta cool this short-timin' ass."
Clunk – *There it is, Holmes.*

Trouble was, there it wasn't:
for the unseen spore found cover beneath the skin
for 27 days, 27 years, more,
sent out long, seeking tendrils around the breastbone,
thickly upward on the last nerve thread,
which hung sickly blossoms from the eyelids
to the eyes, through the visual field,
bringing home loud, baffled pictures to the head:
baby-san by the wire selling sister for *wan dollah*;
mama-san walking armloads of ancestral bones
she dug up under crushed GI beer cans and roach clips;
the same *mama-san* crouched on the smoking rise,
burning half-drums of GI outhouse shit;
rows of faded-green boys at the edge of the strip,
no more jive-talking, for the bags wrap them –
that, and more,
but not about to rob my sleep,
no, not about to rub me raw.
Clunk – *There it is, Holmes.*

Medical Ballistics

The hills around were black-green,
this one mounded in red dirt, scraped clean,
gouged by bulldozers on wide, rusted tracks,
dropped from the sky by windmill choppers.
Sandbags everywhere, stacked around the guns,
banked in the earth for sheltering bunkers –
relief from the sun, buffer for incoming shells.
Night came, and all the clanging day fears
rattled loudly on one slender nerve.
The eyes for the guns scoped the snaking trails and paddies,
pried open the thin cover of darkness
for all things that moved over the foregone vastness of home,
their home, the free-fire zone.

Cassidy sat by the field radio,
took the calls from the eyes in the bush,
plotted the grids, relayed the targeted numbers
that pointed the huge guns
at the flitting shadows in the distant brush.
For a time his hand was steady on the handset,
the voice surefire, the mind lethal-quick on the coordinates.

Back again to the barracks at Lajeune,
late Sunday morning, off-duty boys sleeping in with hangovers,
sounding their hacking matins to the prickly-hot air.
He crept out across the grass lot to the dayroom,
to the shelves of books over the pool table,
pulled down a leather-bound volume on medical ballistics
(how it got there, stuck between Zane Gray and Erskine Caldwell,
one could only guess), leafed through it, for the longest time
studied the photos and illustrations of wounds from bullets,

all calibers and designs, from the shrapnel of grenades,
ragged holes, large ripping bites from the torso, arms, legs.
Enough seen, he closed it with the reverence accorded a hymnal,
and set out on foot toward town, stopping along the way
to watch a backyard boy swinging on a tire-swing,
his bare legs vaulting over an airship cloud,
then pulling back, downswung, grazing the high weeds
before touching, already sprung for the next ascent.

Argyle Street, Chicago

It wasn't raining hard but long enough to run water
    along the curb.
My son and I, the tag-along, walked past McDonald's arches,
past Big Chick's Bar and Rique's Regional Mexican Restaurant,
then turned beneath the big green sign that read *Argyle Street*,
and as we were rounding the corner,
dropped off the map, or so it seemed,
touching down on another land mass, oceans away,
the Vietnam of ghosts all mine, in one short breath:
thickets of signs in wavy strokes and cantilevered characters
hanging from shops and markets for clean-swept city blocks,
and the smells of curry and ginger following us.

He was picking up more lucky bamboo for his apartment,
having been charmed by its simple grace,
exotic character and low maintenance
(no soil, just water, little sun).
The shop was a bamboo-forested alcove
housing shoots of every size, cut and configuration,
all placed in glass planter-bowls and vases,
which gently cupped the floating hair-roots at the base.
A small sign told us *lucky* was for good luck as a gift.
The young shop owner wrapped the stems and roots
in damp paper towels and covered them with plastic
while conversing with us in near-perfect English.
We quick-stepped down the street under dripping awnings.
The rain was coming down harder now,
the runoff rippling higher against the curbstone
and welling into the deep cracks in the walk
from which these proud, straight plants would rise,
given half a chance and a lick of luck.

Kim Phuc

There it was before me,
the one that stung like no other,
the photo snapped in Vietnam '72,
of nine-year-old Kim running
from the napalm that took her infant brothers,
those eyes blank for deposit of our horror,
her clothes as one, fused with the flesh,
fused in our memories, the nakedness,
a different kind of nakedness
for all the world to see, stopping it dead,
stripping the viewer unclean,
a pause like no other,
the blind purchase of innocence and pain,
and the soldiers walking beside her
detached as death itself.

Lives later, her voice heard on the radio,
a meek, lone voice among former foes,
there to complete the story:
how long and hard the fight to save her;
the miracle of healing, of forgiveness;
her wounds a shrine for causes;
her dream of saving others as a doctor;
the joy of bringing forth new life through family;
how after thirty years the scars still hurt,
said with no anger or pity,
despite the indisputable right.

About the Author

~85~

Paul Scollan has spent thirty years as a clinical social worker and administrator at mental health centers. Since college days he has been dog-earing poetry anthologies and jotting lines of his own on the backs of office memos and on mental notepads during sleepless nights and stints in checkout lines. His poetry finds its source in his professional work, his years of travel in Spanish-speaking countries, his experience in the Vietnam War, and the wonderful peculiarities of being from a large Irish-Catholic family. His work, which looks for daylight in small cracks of the walls surrounding us, has appeared in *The Connecticut River Review*, *Oasis Journal*, *Litchfield Review*, and *Sow's Ear*. A native son of Connecticut, Paul lives in Meriden with his wife, Lori Egan-Scollan.

This book is set in Garamond Premier Pro, which had its genesis in 1988 when type-designer Robert Slimbach visited the Plantin-Moretus Museum in Antwerp, Belgium, to study its collection of Claude Garamond's metal punches and typefaces. During the mid-fifteen hundreds, Garamond — a Parisian punch-cutter — produced a refined array of book types that combined an unprecedented degree of balance and elegance, for centuries standing as the pinnacle of beauty and practicality in type-founding. Slimbach has created an entirely new interpretation based on Garamond's designs and on comparable italics cut by Robert Granjon, Garamond's contemporary.

To order additional copies of this book
or other Antrim House titles, contact the publisher at

Antrim House
21 Goodrich Rd., Simsbury, CT 06070
860.217.0023, AntrimHouse@comcast.net
or the house website (www.AntrimHouseBooks.com).

•

On the house website
are sample poems, upcoming events,
and a "seminar room" featuring supplemental biography,
notes, images, poems, reviews, and
writing suggestions.